Easy-To-Make Paper Art Activities for Holidays and Seasons

Katharine Roebken Churchill

INSTRUCTO/McGraw-Hill
Paoli, Pennsylvania 19301

Editor: *Maureen H. Cook*
Illustrations: *Carole Smith*
Cover Design: *Gilbert Lieberman*
Art Assistant: *Mary Casatelli*

Churchill, Katharine Roebken.
  Easy-to-make paper art activities for holidays
and seasons.

  Includes index.
  1. Paperwork — Study and teaching. 2. Creative
activities and seat work. I. Smith, Carole.
II. Title.
TT870.C55   745.54   77-13102
ISBN 0-07-082060-0

DEDICATION

With Love

To my Mother and Father
Who put up with productive messes,
Treasured what I made, and taught
Me anything was possible.

To Patrick
For his enthusiasm, his love
And his help cleaning up.

To all my Students
For their energy and imagination.

And most of all
To Christopher, Keely, Mike, Pat and
Shelly for everything they are.

CONTENTS

A Special Message To Adults Who Use This Book With Children

Most art projects have a life of their own. The adult simply brings them into reality by having materials and equipment handy. He or she must be able to ask children questions that will kindle their imagination.

Children can accomplish many important learning objectives by manipulating paper and constructing objects with it. By using these activities they can:

- Improve coordination of perception with hand movements.
- Develop small muscle control in hands.
- Be given opportunities to make individual choices and decisions as well as encouragement for inventiveness.
- Increase ability to adapt and change process as necessary to accomplish a successful end.

Think of ideas in this book as beginnings — a starting point upon which can be built as many variations as there are people. A successful art activity is one where there are many different solutions. For this reason it is important to encourage children to avoid tracing or slavish copying. It is also very important to praise variety. The artwork produced by each child should be significantly different from that of others in arrangement, color, and detail. Under no circumstances should dittoed sheets or patterns created by an adult be used. Children are naturally creative. The way that *they* interpret their ideas originally is of utmost importance.

All the projects in this book can be made with some variety of paper and simple equipment. In many of the activities, different papers can be substituted with successful results. Since there is never just one way to do any of these ideas, experiment a little with what materials you have available.

You may demonstrate a basic technique and even discuss the possibilities of the materials you've chosen. You may wish to use your sample in your demonstration or instructions but only if you point out it is *your* solution and not the only one. It is not to be copied, but used as a way to understand the construction steps. Emphasize that no two projects should look alike even though they share a common theme, material or technique. Put your sample out of sight after the demonstration.

Encourage children to use "mistakes" as a means of inventing other ways of doing things. Remember, there are no right or wrong answers — just different ones in art.

WHAT IS PAPER?

The dictionary defines paper as a "substance made in the form of thin sheets or leaves, from rags, straw, wood or other fibrous materials, for various uses."

To be classed as true paper, the thin sheets must be made from fiber that has been beaten until each filament is a separate unit.

The fibers most commonly used today are ground wood pulp. The finest papers are made from linen and cotton rags. The only all-rag paper with which most people come in contact is the paper upon which the United States currency is printed.

The beaten fibers are mixed with water and lifted from the water with a screen. As the water drains through the screen, a thin sheet of intertwined fiber is left on the screen's surface. After the fiber dries, it is a sheet of paper.

This was the manner in which Ts'ai Lun formed the first paper — in about 105 A.D. in China. Today's large and efficient papermaking machines employ the same principle.

BLENDER PAPER

For an idea of how paper is made, try this technique. Use recycled paper as the raw material.

You will need:
   A scrap of window screen the size of paper desired, for instance: 8" x 8" or 3" x 5"
   Newspapers, colored comics, junk mail, magazine pictures, old letters, labels, etc.
   Iron, set at "cotton"
   Blender
   Large, shallow, oblong pan (cake pan works well)

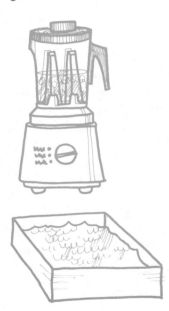

1. Fill blender one-half full of water.
2. Add torn pieces of paper — about the size of a quarter.
3. Add color paper pieces torn the same as above. Control color of paper by using color printed raw materials. For instance, many predominantly red photos add a pink tint to paper.
4. Blend at high speed until finely pureed.
5. Pour into cake pan half full of water. Stir to get fiber floating.
6. Slip screen into mixture.
7. Bring screen up from bottom, catching a layer of mixture on the screen.
8. Let excess drip off.
9. Lay screen on pad of newspapers to soak up water until damp.
10. Place unprinted newsprint or blotting paper over mixture on screen, then iron. Continue ironing sheet as needed. Let sheet cool occasionally. Don't rush this step! When paper is dry, it will lift up easily — with a beautiful deckle edge.

Note: Even young children can do this if ironing is done by an adult!

BASIC MATERIALS — PAPERS

Construction Paper — like its name implies, this is stiff enough to hold its shape or a fold, and flexible enough to do just about anything with except stretch.

Tissue Paper — thin, transparent, and available in deep bright colors as well as pastels. Excellent for collage and soft construction, such as flowers and feathers.

Corrugated Paper — a double-layered paper with the top layer of paper forming a ribbed surface. It is flexible and forms tubes and cones easily. A rigid surface can be created by gluing the corrugated paper back to back with the ribs on one side at right angles to the ribs on the other. Corrugated paper responds well to scoring and can be sculpted. Comes in many bright colors and is very strong.

Crepe Paper — comes in a wide variety of bright colors and some patterns such as brick. Its name comes from the surface texture which resembles crepe and gives this paper the ability to stretch and ruffle. Its strong yet lightweight qualities are fabric-like and make crepe paper a versatile paper.

Typing Paper — this lightweight paper comes in two standard sizes, 8½ x 11 and 8½ x 14 inches. It is usually white, but pastel colors are available. This paper is excellent for paper folding projects, as well as collages and small sculptures.

Tagboard or Poster Board — a medium weight cardboard. Excellent for construction and backgrounds.

Novelty Papers — *Double-hue:* a paper with a different color tone on each side, especially effective for cards or sculpture. *Foil:* a shiny, metallic paper. *Velour:* a paper with a flocked, velvety surface, excellent for decorations.

Found Papers — newspapers, brown bags, wrapping paper, cardboard boxes and cylinders, wallpaper, old watercolor paintings, paper towels and napkins, facial tissues, etc.

Note: It's nice to have a box to keep paper scraps in for future projects.

ADHESIVES

White Glue — an emulsion of polyvinyl acetate. It can be removed with water while sticky, dries clear and is water resistant. It can also be easily thinned with water and applied as a permanent finish.

Rubber Cement — this adhesive does not wrinkle paper. Excess glue rubs off when dry. Best for flat work.

Flour Paste — an old, faithful paste made from flour and water. Mix flour with a small amount of water until you have a smooth paste with no lumps.

Library Paste — a commercial version of flour paste, water soluble and inexpensive.

Masking Tape — a strong, tan-colored tape best for fastening and hanging displays.

Cellophane Tape — a clear, gummed tape good for hinges and fastening.

TOOLS

Scissors   Crayons   Ruler
Stapler   Paints   String
Pencil   Compass   Yarn

BASIC TECHNIQUES

Cutting

Turn paper instead of scissors because it's hard to cut sideways or upside down.

Cut two the same with 2 pieces of paper.

Cut things the same on both sides by cutting on the fold.

Make a shape grow by cutting a spiral.

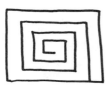 

Fringe

A jagged edge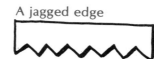

A scalloped edge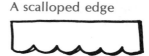

Tearing

Hold fingers close to tear.

Tear a little at a time to control shape.

Many time accidents will suggest new ideas for shapes.

Folding

Paper can be folded on a curved line by scoring with a pointed tool, like a scissors point. Draw the tool firmly along the line where fold is desired, then pinch to fold into shape.

Pleating

Curling

WAYS OF ATTACHING THINGS

Tabs **Slots**

Paper springs

Fold back, one over the other, alternately pressing the folds together.

Stapling

Staple shapes within shapes. Hang or stand. Add a paper base. Or glue shapes onto shapes.

Form strips into shapes by shortening some strips.

Weaving

FORMS AND CONTAINERS

A stapler works fast on these:

Ball **Cone** **Loop** **Cone Hanging Basket**

Open Boxes

Fold paper in half, then in fourths to form an open box.

Cut a piece of construction paper large enough to fit in open corner. Glue or tape for closure and reinforcement.

16 Squares Box

Fold paper in half, twice in each direction, until you have 16 squares. Cut in four places on folds to make tabs. Overlap tabs around corners and paste in place. Add handle and decorate.

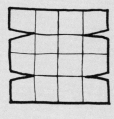
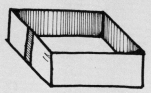
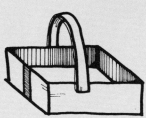

Cylinder

Fold a rectangular shaped paper in shape. Add bottom by cutting circle larger than cylinder, then cutting slits all around just up to the cylinder. Fold tabs up and glue in place — outside or in. Decorate.

Stuffed Forms

These can be large or small. Use two sheets of paper and cut identical shapes. Join edges by gluing, stitching, stapling or taping. Leave an opening (mouth) so form can be stuffed with crumpled newspaper or paper scraps until it is puffy. Decorate. If small, hang as mobiles or place on cardboard stands with V slots cut to hold sculptures.

MOBILES

In balancing, always work from the bottom to the top.

Balance shapes on:
    wires
    pipe cleaners
    cardboard strips
    sticks or dowels
    twigs
    larger shapes

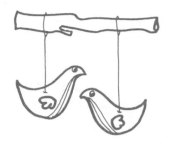

Lay bar across finger until it balances. Tie, glue or staple hanging string from that point.

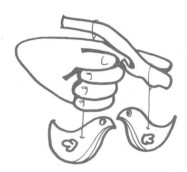

To make many balancing bars on one mobile, attach a balanced section to the next bar. Add more shapes, then find balance point on new bar. See A. Instead of a balance bar, try attaching small shapes to a large one. Find balance point and hang. See B.

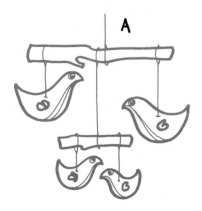

A

B

DIORAMAS

Choose a scene to create. Collect materials (you'll need a cardboard box at least 12″ x 10″ — or bigger). Do you have some plastic figures or models that would be appropriate? Decide if your scene should be an inside or outside scene. Try one of these ways to cut your box to open it up to light.

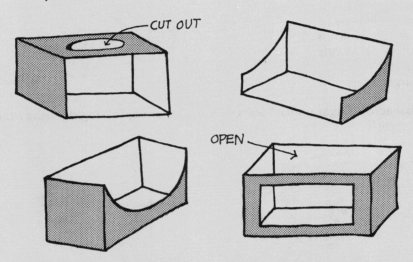

For an Outside Scene:

Try a curved piece of cardboard, paper or tagboard to fit the inside of your box. Make sure it's as high as your box but longer than the back. Staple or tape edges to sides of basic box.

Ground Cover

To get the effect you want, try sprinkling any of the following materials over glue:

sand or dirt
grass clippings
pencil shavings
tiny rocks, shells

fabric, cotton batting
carpet scraps
crumpled paper

Background Techniques

Watercolor. Try a wash for sky and ground areas — let dry before adding more detail. Try a night sky with a moon and stars or a sunset.

Chalk or crayon. Try using the side of these for a soft effect. Try blending colors, fading from light to heavy by pressing lightly or heavily with the chalk or crayon on the paper.

Paper or fabric collage. Cut out or tear shapes needed. Glue in place. Torn paper makes excellent trees, rivers or mountains.

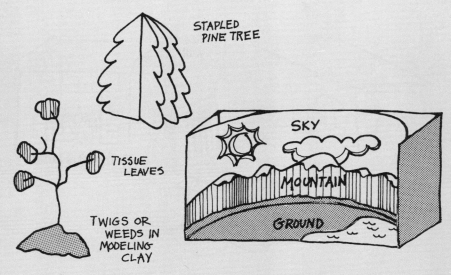

STAPLED PINE TREE

TISSUE LEAVES

TWIGS OR WEEDS IN MODELING CLAY

SKY

MOUNTAIN

GROUND

For An Inside Scene:

Use box as is with corners, but cut light hole in top. Imagine a room before furniture. Strive for realism by adding windows, doors, fireplaces, pictures, etc. Consider wall treatment, floors, even curtains. What real materials, such as carpet, fabric, wallpaper and tile could you use?

Try making a cozy interior with a window through which you can see the outside.

Paper Art Activities

Furniture

Cardboard works fine for furniture. Most can be made from two or three pieces, glued together. Draw in details, add fabric or paper upholstery.

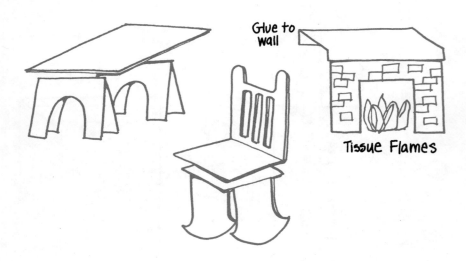

Glue to wall

Tissue Flames

People

Cut out paper dolls. Glue feet to diorama if desired. Dressed clothespins, spools or pipe-cleaner figures make good people.
Use modeling clay, too.

LETTERING

Cut paper into a stack of rectangles of desired size. Make sure they are all the same size.

Cut outside edges. Fold to cut centers out.

If more than one of the same letter is needed, cut 2 or 3 at the same time.

Visualize most of the letter touching all edges of the rectangle, then cut away unwanted part.

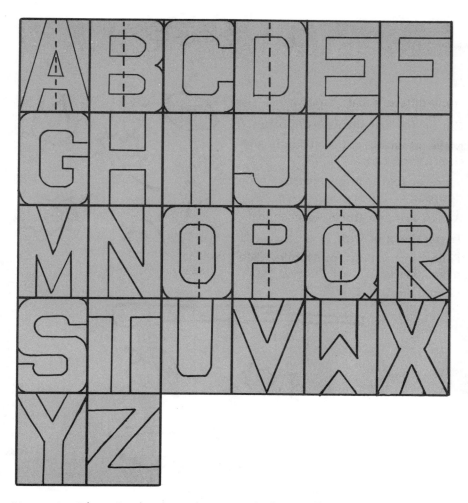

Note: Avoid pasting letters to form words diagonally or vertically, as these directions often make reading difficult.

SEPTEMBER

LEAF MOBILES

Study different leaf shapes.

Cut or tear leaf shapes from paper.

Make as many different kinds and sizes as you can.

Score or fold leaf to suggest veins if desired.

Attach string or thread to each leaf.

Tie to a twig or wire.

Follow instructions for Mobiles. (See page 15.)

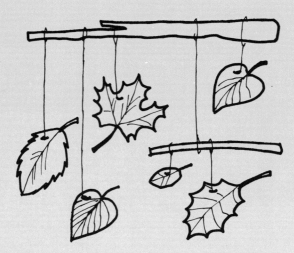

CROSSWORD PUZZLE

Make cardboard squares. Add a cut paper letter on each square. (See page 19.)

Assign a number value to each letter for keeping score.

Deal out seven cards to each player. Put other cards face down. Players draw from pile when necessary. (Game can be played by individual.)

Make as many words as you can by fitting them together "crossword style".

Letter squares can also be made by cutting printed letters from magazines.

BOOK JACKETS

Make book jackets from brown bags or wrapping paper.

Lay book open on a cut-open bag. Trim to fit, leaving three inches on each end to fold around book cover.

Cut out large letters to glue on jacket.

Decorate with title or name.

Turn letters into pictures by adding more paper parts.

Try initial designs and cut letters. Repeat design.

Try alternating colors. Glue some letters backwards or upside down for symmetrical effect.

Symmetry

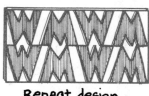

Repeat design

Letter picture

JAPANESE FOLDING BOOK

Pages of the book can be made from drawing, wrapping or shelf paper.

Fold a long strip of paper lengthwise.

Then fold accordion style to form the pages.

 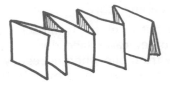

Cut two cardboard covers from tagboard or shirt boards. The covers should be ¼" larger on all edges than the size of the pages.

Decorate the cardboard by covering with colored paper, tissue collage, wallpaper scraps, or magazine photo montage. Try a "paper leather" effect using brown paper bags, painted with brown watercolor and crumpled to make wrinkles. Smooth out to dry. Mitre corners.

Glue book covers to end pages.

Use the pages to write a story, a poem or keep a diary.

JUMPING JACK SCARECROW

Cut shapes from cardboard:
Body
Two arms
Two legs

Keep shapes large and simple.

You will need to punch two holes in the arms and legs.

Attach arms and legs to body with fasteners.

Tie four strings - one to each limb.

Carefully knot arm strings as shown.

Then knot leg strings to arm string, letting the rest dangle down for pull.

Knot end.

Add fringe for straw.

Decorate with paper cutouts and jump away!

PUMPKIN PATCH

Cut pumpkin's basic shape.
Make 3-D by cutting a slit about halfway into pumpkin. Overlap the two cut edges, forming a shallow cone. Staple or glue together.
Add cut-paper ribs and stem. Add spiral vines with lots of leaves.

SELF-PORTRAIT COLLAGE

Cut head shape. Add features.

Use a mirror to help you "see" yourself or have a friend tell you special things about yourself.

Add body shape, arms and legs. Add clothes to body. Use as many techniques as possible. Tear, curl, fringe, fold, etc. Glue everything together.

Hang the collage.

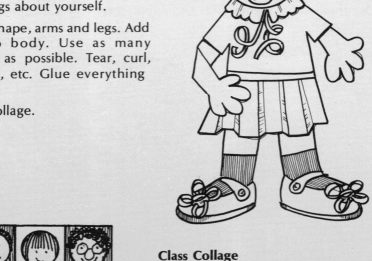

Class Collage

Guess "Who Is Who?" using each child's head. Add facial features. Mount heads on differently colored paper for patchwork effect.

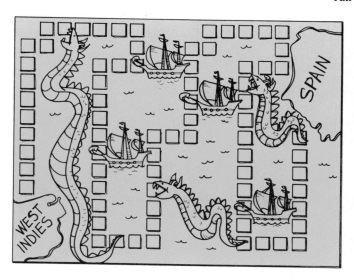

OCTOBER — COLUMBUS DAY
COLUMBUS DAY GAME
A Version of Snakes and Ladders — For 2 to 4 Players

For the gameboard, use a large piece of paper or cardboard. Cut contrasting colored paper into one-inch squares. Glue into a pattern, back and forth across the board as shown — pattern can vary.

Cut out or draw and paste some sea serpents and ships on gameboard. Place serpents so they touch a square in one place and lead backwards to another square elsewhere on the board.

Place ships so they lead on (ahead) to another square on the board.

Cut one-inch diameter circles in different colors for markers for each player.

For the game instructions:

Make 24 paper rectangles 1" x 2" and write numbers 1 to 5 on them.

You may want to write "No Turn" on some rectangles.

Stack these cards face down.

Place circle markers in "Spain".

Players set out on their voyages — moving ahead as many squares as the card drawn tells them.

If player comes to a sea serpent, player slides back; if player comes to a ship, player sails ahead to where it points.

The first one to reach the West Indies wins.

Reshuffle cards if they are used up before game is over.

HALLOWEEN

TRICK OR TREAT BAGS

Use a large, brown grocery bag, double weight if possible. Fold top about two inches down into inside.

Glue into place.

Use another bag to cut a four-inch-wide, 12- to 18- inch-long paper strip.

Fold strip in half lengthwise and glue to make a double-strong handle.

Staple handle at least twice on each side of bag to attach firmly. Cover any printing on bag with colored paper and decorate with spooky cutout pictures.

Remember as you decorate that the bag has four sides.

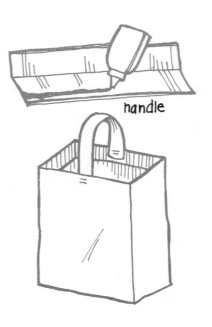

handle

HAUNTED HOUSES

Choose two contrasting colors of paper — each the same size. Cut out a silhouette of an old house with lots of roof peaks, a porch, chimney, and dormer windows.

Draw windows and doors.

Cut around three sides of the doors and windows, leaving the fourth side as a hinge.

Paste on background paper being careful not to put glue on opening parts.

Draw or paste pictures of ghosts, cats, spiders and monsters behind each window and door.

Add clouds, bats, moon and witches in the sky.

Close doors and windows to surprise someone when they're opened.

TORN-PAPER SHAPES . . .
. . . can make spooky cats, witches and monsters.

Cat

Tear circles.

Add ears, face, legs, whiskers.

Tear a question-mark shape for cat's tail.

Witch

Face can be life-size.

Tear face shapes, hair, hat.

Add expression to face with eyebrows.

Count

Wolfman

Hint: Always put pupils in eyes to let them "see".

To make a door decoration, add a crumpled crepe-paper "body" and torn-paper hands.

SKELETONS

Refer to a chart or model of human bone structure.

Use three, 12″ x 18″ pieces of white drawing paper or light tagboard folded in half.

Sketch parts of skeleton as shown.

Cut out.

Add black paper behind cutout features.

Glue together or attach parts with paper fasteners.

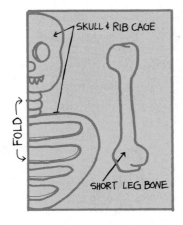

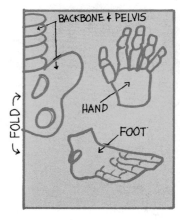

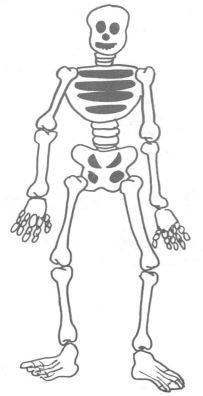

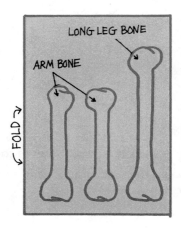

Note: Follow this craft with some figure drawing.

SCARY SCULPTURES

Stuff a paper sack, crepe or tissue paper with newspaper, cloth, crumpled scraps, etc.

Spiders

Make form so end makes small head.

Tape or tie.

Add pleated paper legs (remember — 8 legs).

Jack-O'-Lantern

Tied top becomes stem.

Glue on cut paper face.

Owls

Ghosts

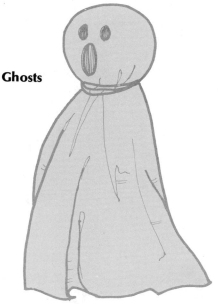

COSTUMES

These costumes and masks when made from corrugated paper or tagboard are remarkably durable and very attractive. They will wear well through a dress rehearsal and half a dozen performances or a vigorous night of "Trick or Treat".

The costumes can be easily made by children. Once the basic costume is cut out, it can be used as a pattern to make many more. Children are especially expert at inventing eye-catching designs to decorate costumes.

Basic Costumes

Create a vest-like cylinder using corrugated paper or poster board. Make sure the ribs of the corrugated paper are vertical and that the cylinder has a small overlap at back.

Using a model to help assure fit, cut large armholes at sides. Allow 2" to 3" at shoulder. This area can be reinforced with masking tape if necessary.

Cut a "V" for the neck so that the cylinder is comfortable to wear.

Cut scallops or zigzags at bottom end if desired.

Put on costume and use masking tape to hold the back together.

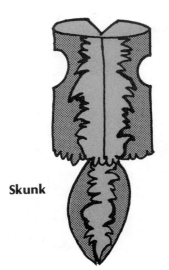

Skunk

Animals

Begin with basic costume.

Staple or glue a tail in place.

For a tail that hangs gracefully, make sure the corrugated ribs are horizontal on tail.

Decorate with appropriate strips or spots cut from contrasting construction paper and pasted to costume.

PAPER THIN STRIPS OR PAPER STRAWS FOR NEEDLES

TISSUE PAPER TAIL

Porcupine

Rabbit

Giraffe

For head, use tagboard cut on fold and glued to top of cylinder. Try drawing, painting, or use paper features and spots.

Four-Legged Body

Use a box large enought for two bodies. Add mask. Add other features. (See *Cylinder Mask*, page 32.)

Birds and Fish

Begin with basic costume.

For rigid tail use two pieces of corrugated paper glued together with corrugated ribs vertical. Place tail through slit in body. Tape well.

Scales

Try adding foil for shine on fish scales.

Wings

Make wings for arms by adding yarn ties or stapled corrugated paper strips.

Arm goes through loops.

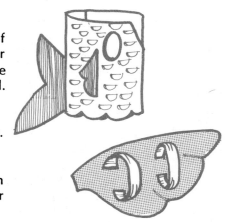

SHALLOW CONE MASKS

Use basic circle with slit to create basic shallow cone. (See page 33.)

Corrugated paper, tagboard, or even construction paper (if not for heavy use) can be used to make masks.

Try varying cone depth for longer noses and heads like those of mice.

Overlap and staple.

Find and cut eyeholes.

Add yarn ties or headband to keep on head.

Decorate with cut paper.

Use pipe cleaners or straws for whiskers.

CYLINDER MASK

Make a paper cylinder large enough to fit over head to shoulders.

Cut eyeholes and shoulder curves.

Add facial features using any kind of available paper for ears, nose, mouth.

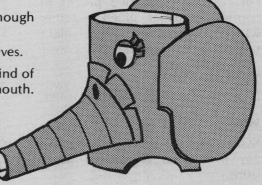

PAPER BAG MASKS

Cut eyeholes. Add other features, such as beak, nose, ears.

Add crepe paper or tissue fur or feathers. Start pasting "feather or fur" fringe at bottom and work up. Overlap a little each row.

Use yarn or masking tape to gather neck if desired.

HATS

Cylinders

Roll a rectangle of corrugated paper into size of cylinder needed. Staple together. Decorate.

Brim can be added by slicing circle in center like a pie and pushing over top cylinder. (See page 14.)

Cones

Peaked cone is made from a rectangle of corrugated paper twisted into a cone and trimmed at base to form a curve.

Shallow cone is made from a circle with a slit to the center. Overlap edges and staple. Add yarn ties.

Crowns

Staple or glue cylinders. Cut shapes. Add paper jewels.

WIGS AND BEARDS

Add corrugated paper or paper "braids" or curls to a headband or shallow cone "hat". Add yarn ties.

CREPE PAPER BEARD

PAWS, CLAWS AND FEET

Try adding corrugated paper claws to gloves or mittens with tape. (Tagboard works, too.)

Make corrugated paper spats or tagboard feet.

Add a strip for ankle.

Tape on or punch holes to tie to shoelace.

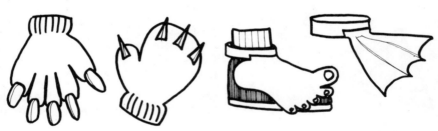

WRAPPING PAPER PONCHOS

Fold paper and cut headhole.
Reinforce edges with masking tape.
Decorate.

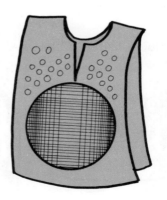

NOVEMBER — THANKSGIVING

TISSUE TURKEYS

Make turkey body by folding and cutting 8 squares of tissue paper. (Bigger squares make bigger turkeys.)

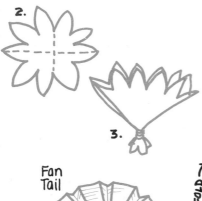

Open and separate each shape. Grasp in the center and twist each one.

Use glue to attach the twisted paper shapes together at narrow ends to make ball.

Fan Tail

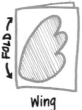

Wing

Wattle

Cut a colored paper tail or make a paper fan for a tail or try separate large tail feathers.

Add tail to cover twisted area of body. Fan tail.

Cut head, neck and wings and glue in place on tissue. Don't forget wattle!

Flatten bottom so that turkey can sit on a flat surface.

CYLINDER TURKEYS

Staple or glue paper into the size cylinder desired. Make cylinders narrow with fat loops.

Cut wings and tail; attach with tabs.

Make a loop head. Cut diamond shape for beak. Add eyes using tabs.

Attach head to body with paper neck.

Add details using many paper sculpture techniques. (See pages 11-12.)

CYLINDER PILGRIMS AND INDIANS

Use 9″ x 12″ sheet of paper for cylinder body.

Pilgrim's hat could be a circle with slices cut then slipped over cylinder. Make headband with feathers for male Indians. Remember, no feathers for females!

Cut arms on fold and they will be both alike.

Cut out slice of cylinder to make pants or legs. Or attach a paper skirt.

Add details using many paper sculpture techniques. (See pages 11-12.)

PILGRIMS' COSTUMES

Corrugated paper makes an excellent material for costumes.

Hats

Use cylinders of paper.

Add circle brim (see page 14), band and buckle.

Bonnets

Use 12" by 18" paper.

Fold long edge back about 3".

Cut 1" wide slits in other end about 6" long.

Gather strips and staple together.

Add yarn ties.

Collars and Cuffs

Add paper collars and cuffs to regular clothes. Attach with tape.

Skirts

Long skirts and aprons can be made from crepe paper. Simply gather skirt on a sturdy strip of tagboard and glue. Add apron. Tape on to wear.

INDIANS' COSTUMES

The male woodland Indians that ate Thanksgiving dinner with the Pilgrims often wore leggings and loincloths.

Add fringe made from crepe or wrapping paper to jeans or slacks. Pin or tape into place.

Add paper loincloth attached to belt or a tagboard strip. Attach with tape around waist.

Crepe-paper wigs can be made with strips of paper glued to heavier paper — strips could be braided or tied with yarn. Attach with bobby pin.

Female woodland Indians wore long leather gowns which can easily be made from crepe paper similar to a poncho (see page 34) and tied at waist. Cut hole for head. Tie with yarn. Cut fringe. Add paper beads cut from colored paper.

CUT FRINGE

GLUE HERE

CUT PAPER BEADS

GLUE HERE

CREPE PAPER BRAIDS

THANKSGIVING DIORAMA

Choose an open box (see page 16).

Prepare ground with texture glued on. Use:

> sand
> pencil shavings
> grass clippings
> torn tissue

Add cardboard tables with tiny paper food (see page 18).

Animals

People

Paper-doll cutouts. Fold feet to stand and glue down. (Especially good for tiny figures and where you need many.)

Pipe-cleaner frame or *stick figure.* Add paper clothes or pad figure with crepe paper, tissue, etc.

Stand these figures in a pinch of modeling clay.

Shelters

Fold paper to create small boxes. (See page 13.) Cut out or add doors and windows. Use strips of birch-bark-marked paper. Glue, tab or tape.

COLLAGE CORNUCOPIAS

Good for a group project, for a bulletin board or for an individual project. They make nice shadow boxes if glued into shallow boxes.

Try tearing the curved horn shape. Think of a pear or a yellow crooked necked squash. Cut if you wish.

Tear or cut fruit and vegetable shapes and glue in place. Try arranging all shapes first before gluing into final position.

For a 3-D version, glue some shapes into shallow cones by making a slit to the middle and overlapping a bit. Apples, oranges and grapes can be done this way.

Try tearing a curved line from a darker colored paper to accent opening. Glue in place.

Score a banana shape to fold on a curve. Corrugated paper is excellent for this.

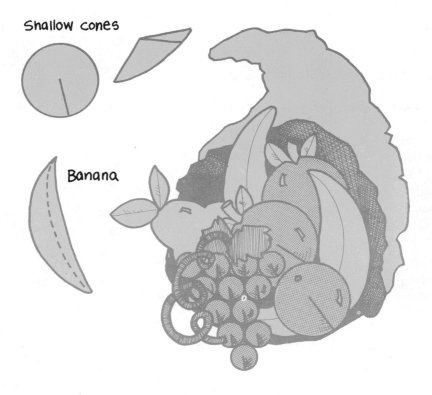

Shallow cones

Banana

INDIAN SYMBOLGRAMS

Use tissue paper for transparent effects; colored paper for solid colors. Experiment with found papers for unusual textures. Research Indian symbols and beadwork. Choose some to create a pleasing design - symbols can tell a story or represent a "monogram" of a name.

Try repeating shapes and colors.

Use contrasts in color and textures.

Vary size.

Brown-bag backgrounds might be very suitable.

HIBERNATING ANIMALS

Use folded paper to make backbone or basic shape. Add details after cutting design.

Or use stuffed paper technique with two pieces of paper (see page 14). Stitch or glue leaving a part open.

Try torn tail for squirrel. Score to make it stay up.

Draw point of scissors down tail. Pinch to fold on scored line.

Stuff, then complete closing.

Note: These can be used on tables, in murals or diorama.

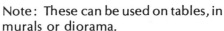

DECEMBER — HANUKKAH

FESTIVAL OF LIGHTS

To create a Menorah candelabrum, cut on fold after drawing.

Cut candle shapes from contrasting colors.

Remember 9 candles. The center one is lit first. Add flames as candles are lit — one each day.

Glue parts together on to a large background sheet. To make picture stand for display on a table, simply fold picture back down center.

Note: 3-D twists of tissue make nice flames.

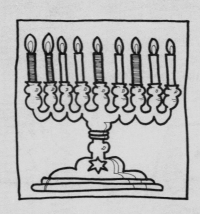

CHRISTMAS
PEACE DOVE

PINCH AT EDGE

Begin by rolling the short edges of a rectangle together. Make a small pinch on one edge of the center.

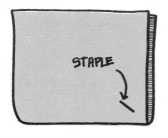

STAPLE

Keeping the rest rolled, staple diagonally about 3" inches from pinch mark (this will become the beak).

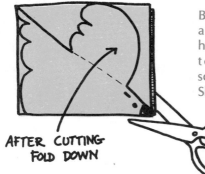

AFTER CUTTING
FOLD DOWN

Begin cutting diagonally slightly above and toward the staple to create head. Then curve neck back around to make rounded wings. Add scallops, or fringe edge, for feathers. Shape a tail.

Fold down wings.

Add beak, eyes and olive branch.

Find balance point and hang from string. Hang around room or arrange in a mobile (see page 15). Make tiny peace doves and arrange on a tree.

Hang around room.

CHRISTMAS TREE MOBILE

Cut two identical shapes and sandwich a string or thread between them, gluing in place. Try two different colors of green, then decorate with cut-paper ornaments.

For a fancier version, cut two more tree shapes, then cut into parts (thirds work well).

Space parts along string. (Make sure there is a front and back to each part.)

Glue both sides to string.

Try tinfoil glued onto one side of tree before cutting for sparkle.

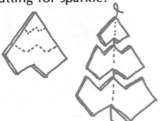

SLOTTED BELLS

Use a lighter weight paper like typing, poster or wrapping paper.

Fold an 8½" square to make an X.

Fold again to make a **+**.

Fold entire piece into one triangle. Round off bottom edge of triangle.

Continue cutting parallel curves up the triangle on every other side but never all the way through fold. Make cuts about ¼" apart.

Open carefully and pull center of circle up to make bell shape.

Add clapper or star if desired.

Hang by thread.

Add glitter to edge of bell for special touch.

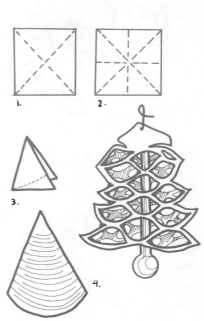

44

CONE DECORATIONS

Make basic cones the sizes desired (see page 33).

If you make any of these decorations small, add a string and hang in branches of your Christmas Tree.

Make sure you scale features and extras to fit.

For Angel: Use pastel colors.

Fold two pieces of paper in half. Cut wings from one; arms and sleeves from the other. Paste to cone.

Cut eyes, mouth, and strips for hair. (Curl the strips.)

Put a candle, book or gift in hands if desired. Decorate with stars, ruffled edges, sparkles, etc.

For Santa: Round off back points of cone if Santa is to stand alone.

Cut beard from a triangle of paper.

Use paper scraps for eyes, nose and hat tassle.

Add paper loop for hat rim.

Add paper-strip arms.

Use eyebrows to create an expression.

For Reindeer: Turn basic cone up-side down.

Fold paper for ears for 3-D effect, or cut into edge of cone to make ear and pinch forward. Don't forget pupils for eyes.

Add antlers, eyes, and nose.

GINGERBREAD COOKIES

Draw outline of a rounded human form.

Cut out and paste on white paper.

Trim, leaving a little white "icing" edge around "cookie".

Add eyes, mouth buttons and hang with thread.

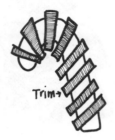

Trim→

CANDY CANES

Cut canes and strips of paper for contrasting candy stripes.

Paste stripes diagonally on canes.

Trim excess paper. String.

LOOPS

Cut multicolored strips in varying widths and lengths. Paste or staple into curved shapes and loops. Add string or ribbon.

ICICLES

Glue foil to construction paper. Cut into icicle shapes.

Cut out circles, then cut into spirals. Hang by thread. Add glitter.

STARS

Foil Star

Cut a 5-pointed star from foil. Hang from string.

Soda Straw Star

Tie with thread in center. Bend rays out.

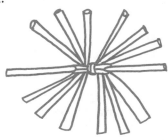

Eight-Pointed Star

Begin with two squares — any size. (Even typing paper works for this one.) Fold to make a X and then a +.

Cut only halfway to center on the crossfolds of each square. Fold each of the eight flaps towards the X fold.

Paste stars back to back to make an eight-pointed sparkle.

Tie with thread in center.

Bend rays out.

Try using contrasting colors of paper and/or foil.

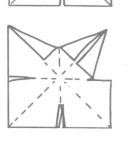

TABLE DECORATIONS

Reindeer

Fold a rectangular piece of paper in half.

Draw the outline of the reindeer, using fold for back. Cut shape leaving fold intact.

Cut slot for antlers.

Add eyes, nose, ears, and antlers.

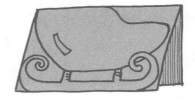

Make a sleigh (using the folded paper technique), eight reindeer, and a Santa. Arrange in a winter sky on a bulletin board, or stand on a table.

Pine Tree

Fold three pieces of paper in half lengthwise. (Try three different colors.)

Staple along the fold two or three times. (Make sure staples are in fold.)

Cut a diagonal line lengthwise and then cut branches. Do not cut a trunk.

Fold open and decorate using a paper punch, stars or cut-paper shapes.

String may be added to top to hang.

GIFT WRAPPING

Wrap package with tissue, wrapping paper, or even newspaper (choose from the person's favorite section — comics, sports, fashion, theater, etc.)

Decorate with cut paper or sculpture appropriate to the season or suited to the interests of the person who will receive the gift.

Or turn the whole package into a sculpture or animal.

Try paper flowers instead of bows.

Try paper strips as "ribbon", pleated, curled or looped.

Try tissue paper collage designs forming a repeat pattern.

Cut out large letters. Paste a message on package.

CHRISTMAS COSTUMES

Use corrugated paper to make basic costume tubes. (See page 30.) Vest-length is a good length to wear. Decorate using colored construction paper.

Elves

Use a cone hat.

Add stars or flowers and pointed ears.

Toy Soldiers

Cut strips of construction paper for suspenders and belt.

Add paper feather and stars to cylinder hat.

Jack-In-The-Box (Clown)

Tissue tassle on top of cone hat.

Add tie strings and a fringed collar.

Dolls

Attach crepe paper or curled paper to hat band for curled hair.

Coats

Use longer tubes if coat tails are desired.

Note: You can use roll paper for basic costume, but it is not durable as corrugated paper.

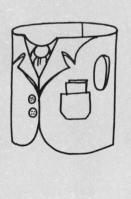
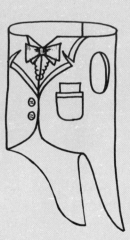

JANUARY — NEW YEAR'S EVE
HATS AND NOISEMAKERS

Make cones or cylinders for hats. Add brims if desired (see pages 14 and 33).

Decorate with tissue or crepe-paper tassels and cutout designs.

Roll small tight cones for horns. Add fringe.

These make a nice display on a "HAPPY NEW YEAR" bulletin board. Put up to greet your students after vacation.

CLOCKS WITH MOVABLE HANDS

Use a paper plate or cut a circle from tagboard.

Draw face and numerals on plate. Or make a cut-paper face and paste to paper plate. Draw numerals on the face.

Punch a small hole in center of plate.

Cut hands for clock from tagboard — keep hands thick. Remember to make one long and one short. Attach hands with brass paper fastener through hole in center.

Try attaching to cardboard circle and hanging on wall.

Or attach to a cardboard box and add a pendulum. It could be cut out or just pasted on the box.

Try making a tagboard clock with large tabs to help it stand.

3-D CRAYON BATIK SNOW SCENES

Begin with two sheets of white drawing paper, crayons and watercolors. On one sheet, use the side of a white crayon to "wax" the surface of the paper, pressing harder in some places than others. Make sure all the area is not covered by crayon. This is the "snow" sheet.

Paint with watercolors — blues and lavenders. Crinkle up, then smooth out to damp dry on newspapers.

On the second sheet use crayons to create a horizon line about halfway down and across the paper fading from yellow, yellow-orange, orange, red to red-violet. Press hard. Paint over with watercolor to make watercolor sunset. This is the "sky" sheet.

When both sheets of watercolor are dry, cut scallops or jagged edges in top of snow sheet for horizon line of mountains or hills. Apply glue to this edge and attach to sky sheet about two-thirds of the way up. Do not try to smooth out the "snow" sheet. The bumps make snowy hills and valleys.

Cut out paper trees with dark bare branches, pine trees, snow people, houses and farms. Arrange on snow and glue in place.

WINTER DIORAMAS

Choose a box (see page 16).

Decide on the type of winter scene you wish to create — rural or urban, interior or exterior.

Paper inside walls for background and sky. Try overlapped tissue colors for a sunset. Paste silver stars on background for night scene. Add middle ground band — trees and buildings.

Add foreground figures — people, animals, cars, snow, sleds, etc.

Trees can be real twigs set in a bit of modeling clay or cut out of paper (see page 16).

Try salt glued on paper for sparkle.

Cover outside for finished look.

PAPER FIGURE

COTTON OR TISSUE SNOW

WINTER FIGURES

Decide on a winter activity, such as skating, sledding or skiing.

Make a wide, basic cone for coat or jacket. (A short cone is more jacket-like.) Add strip for arms. Add hands or mittens.

Cut out head shape and attach to coat. Decorate with hair, face features, cap or scarf.

Attach legs — these can be strips of paper or cardboard.

Add feet and appropriate sports equipment or outfits. Decorate with stripes and designs, buttons, fringe, or tassels.

Bend head, arms, and legs to show action.

These figures can be large (18" high) or very tiny (4" high). Older children enjoy the challenge fine work requires.

Try tiny skaters on a mirror or tinfoil pond. Use bits of clay for feet, or pin skaters on a bulletin board "rink".

LOOP SNOWFLAKE MOBILES

Cut strips of paper in white and icy colors.

Glue small loops together and to each other.

Build a pointed snowflake from center out. The loops can be in a variety of sizes, but it is important to keep sides or points equal.

Hang from string.

A frosting of glitter or spray paint might be appealing.

SNOW FIGURE MOBILE

Cut body snowballs by folding paper and cutting circles in pairs. Cut three pairs of circles in decreasing sizes.

Cut a hat or stocking cap the same way so there are two pieces.

Assemble on a long string.

Sandwich string between pairs of circles, gluing together.

Add "coal" pieces for eyes and buttons; add "carrot" nose, (a very narrow cone), scarf, twig arms. Try glued-on raisins for "coal" and cotton glued to circles for fluff.

Note: Remember to decorate both sides.

SNOW FIGURE STAND-UP

Use a discarded tube for armature. Trim to size if necessary, leaving part of tube for top hat.

Crumple facial tissues or paper toweling and paste to tube to create fluffy balls of "snow".

Paint or cover exposed tube with paper to make a hat. Cut a paper circle for brim, cutting slits evenly in center so brim will slide onto tube.

Use paper punch "coal" to make face.

Use fabric scraps or fringed paper to make scarf and paper broom.

Glue to circle base to stand.

FEBRUARY — VALENTINE'S DAY

PLACE MATS

Use one large sheet of 12" x 18" construction paper for the bottom part of the mat.

Make a lacy top layer from newsprint or typing paper, cutting on folds. Decorate another way by adding cutout love birds, hearts or cut-paper letters.

Or weave a paper place mat. Cut strips of different widths and colors. Fringe or scallop edges of sheet of construction paper. Fold in half. Cut curly or zigzag lines from fold to about ½" from edges. Weave in strips. (Recycled strips of doubled-over newspaper or brown bags could be used for a rustic effect.)

HEART-SHAPED VALENTINE BASKETS

Use two rectangular pieces of paper (9" x 12").

Fold in half and round off a corner.

Place together to make heart.

Paste in place.

Decorate with small hearts and flowers or lovebirds.

Add a handle or a bow or both.

Fill with valentines.

HEART MOBILES

Try one made from strips stapled into heart shapes and glued on string.

Staple strings together at A. Bend B and C ends down and staple together. Arrange on string.

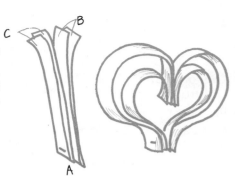

Cut hearts in pairs. Sandwich string between pairs and arrange with space between each pair along string. Try using two colors of paper so color changes occur as hearts swirl on the string or paste smaller hearts on larger hearts — try three on one. Cut out the center of a heart or make a lace heart.

WOVEN HEART

Cut a large heart on folded paper. Use a ruler and pencil to mark lines from fold to about one inch to edge. Cut along those lines. Then weave in one-inch strips of different colored paper.

Paste down edges.

Add string hanger.

LOVEBIRDS

Cut corrugated paper or tagboard into two matching bird shapes by folding the paper and cutting two at once.

Make a fantail by folding tissue or typing paper into accordion pleats. Staple at one end. Glue tail to bird.

Make wings twice as long as the bird.

Cut a slot in the bird's body and slip wings through.

Add eyes on both sides (maybe heart-shaped eyes).

Find the balance point and hang by a string.

Now make another. Hang in pairs.

TOPIARY TREES

For a nice display, try these.

Cut a circle from construction paper for tree top's basic form.

Cut tissue hearts. Decorate tree tops with hearts.

Try small cut squares of tissue paper twisted into puffs and glued to background for a leafy look.

Or try glued on popcorn.

Use paper strips for stems or trunk.

Cut flower pots from paper.

Decorate with strips of ribbon.

Let shapes stick out from tree top by adding glue only to centerfold and letting sides stick out and up.

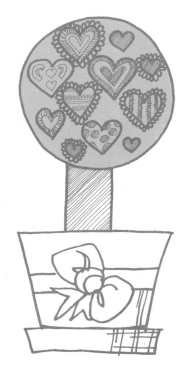

FRIENDSHIP WEEK PAPER DOLLS

Use long rectangular paper 12" x 18" or 9" x 12". Fold in accordion pleats so that each part is exactly touching the next folded edge. The more folds — the more people.

Use a pencil or a crayon to draw the outline of a person — make sure hands touch edges of sides.

Cut out figure through all layers but *do not* cut apart hands.

Open up and add cut-paper hair and faces.

Make each person different.

Try a border of these all around a classroom wall or outlining a bulletin board.

CARDBOARD TUBE CHERRY TREE AND AX

Use a discarded cardboard tube or make one from corrugated paper. Cut four narrow "pie-shaped" slices into top of tube and bend out to make branches.

For leaves, try crumpled roll paper, tissue or drawing paper. Use crayons or paints to decorate. Try crayoned bark texture.

Glue ball of leaves to the fork of branches.

Cut out or use paper-punch cherries to glue on the leaves.

Cut a tiny hatchet out of colored paper. Cut a slot in trunk of tree and slip hatchet into slot.

Trees can be hung by string or pinned to a bulletin board in an orchard scene.

PRESIDENTS' DAY

PRESIDENTS' DAY FIGURES

Roll 3 or 4 newspaper sheets into firm, hard tubes. Add tape to ends and center.

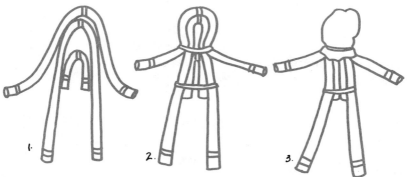

Bend and combine tubes until basic figure is made.

Tie or tape.

Squash to form face and cover with crepe paper. Tie or tape to neck.

Bend to create joints.

Add distinguishing features — face, hair, beard, wig, etc.

Make appropriate crepe-paper clothing. Glue in place.

Place in a tableau or diorama of an important event. Or do all the Presidents.

Note: These figures can be covered with papier-mâché for a more permanent figure.

MARCH
LIONS AND LAMBS

Use basic folded paper to make animal bodies (9″ x 12″ works well). Larger sizes need a paper brace.

Cut out area between legs and under necks.

Lion

Cut out a mane and a tail. Try a torn shape for the mane. Cut slits in mane to slip over head.

Try using tissue glued to basic mane. For a full effect, twist or pleat.

Glue tail to body. Add eyes and nose.

Lamb

Add curls or kinky strips of paper to make a woolly coat for lamb (or glue on cotton tufts).

Add ears and eyes.

ST. PATRICK'S DAY
PARADE BANNERS

Use large sheets of wrapping paper to make basic banner shape.

Fold over to edge and paste to back. Stiffen folded edge with cardboard or dowel.

Fringe or scallop lower edge.

Decorate with designs and symbols to celebrate "Wearing O' The Green " — stripes, shamrocks, leprechauns, rainbows, and lettering.

Hang on walls and/or carry in parade by hanging by string from a broomstick.

SHAMROCK LEPRECHAUNS

Cut medium-sized heart shapes in appropriate colors.

Paste three to a stem of paper to make shamrock.

Turn the shamrock upside down to turn it into a leprechaun.

Add head to stem.

Add hat, face, hands, and boots.

Make several in different sizes.

Leprechauns can hang from strings or can be glued to a spring (two strips of paper woven together — see page 12).

KITES

Take a rectangle of paper and fold in half lengthwise.

Fold each top corner to center.

Fold between A and B (on both sides).

Trim excess that goes beyond lengthwise center fold. Glue down if necessary.

Decorate finished kites with cut-on-fold symmetrical designs. A collage made of tissue paper decorates the kite nicely.

Add string tail, twist tissue or tie-dyed napkins for tail.

These make good bulletin board displays or mobiles. Make a carp or butterfly kite using the stuffed-paper method (see page 14).

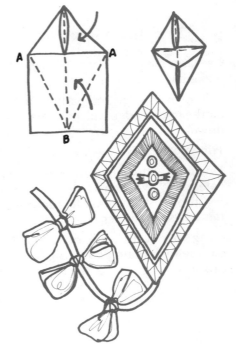

PINWHEELS

  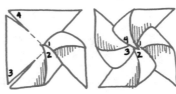

Cut paper into a square.

Fold on diagonals to make an "X".

Try to decorate before assembling.

Cut two-thirds of the way to the center along each fold.

Take alternating corners and curve to center. (They are labeled 1, 2, 3, 4.)

Cut a small circle of tagboard for center of pinwheel.

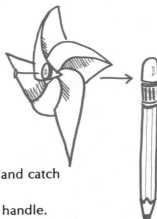

Pierce center of circle with a straight pin and catch each point of the wheel.

Press into pencil, twig or small dowel for handle.

Provide your own wind.

Let parts fit loosely so they will turn easily.

WIND MOBILES

Begin with a circle of paper or try using a shallow cone (see page 33) or a paper plate.

Create a face for the "wind" using cut paper. Think about what kind of a wind you want — fierce winter wind, brisk kite-flying wind, or soft summer breeze.

Use circles or tiny shallow cones for cheeks. Consider eyebrows and size of eyes to create an expression. Add curled strips of different sizes for puffs of air.

Add string to hang.

KALEIDOSCOPE DESIGNS

Create a repeat design collage by cutting many similar shapes in a variety of colors and sizes. (Always make a pair of shapes.)

Begin attaching shapes to each other or to a background paper, repeating the pattern from the center out.

These can be hung or used as greeting cards.

FINGER PUPPETS

Make basic cylinders to fit fingers.

Staple at top.

Add features desired — faces, hands, feet.

Have a Show!

Lion

Lamb

cotton for wool

Kite flyer

Weather person

STORYBOOK STICK PUPPETS

Choose a storybook character to make. Using colored construction paper, cut a body shape (this can be as simple as a rectangle or oval). Glue to a cardboard strip or popsicle stick. Add head, arms and legs, and details. Add props for storytelling. Use them to recreate the story.

LITTLE RED RIDING HOOD

3 LITTLE PIGS

WIZARD OF OZ

APRIL

RAIN CLOUDS

Cut two clouds and glue together leaving an opening (see page 14). Stuff with crumpled newspaper. Cut paper raindrops. Hang raindrops from clouds with string.

UMBRELLAS

Cut top shape of umbrella and add handle.

Cut raindrops and/or flowers to hang from strings coming from umbrella top.

If raindrops and flowers are cut two at a time, they can be glued together with the string between.

A group of tiny umbrellas, or rain clouds could be balanced on wires or stick for a larger effect.

Remember, balance from the bottom up (see page 15)!

COSTUMES FOR SPRING PLAYS

Cutout Masks

Cut out outline desired. Then cut pie-shaped slits to open up an area large enough to fit over face. Remove center except for short flaps to allow for movement.

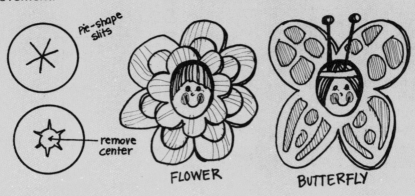

FLOWER   BUTTERFLY

Trees

Make basic costume in a cylinder shape taller than person. Cut holes for face and arms.

Make large branches by rolling paper into long cylinders. Make sure two of the branches are wide enough to fit over arms.

Make small branches by rolling smaller cylinders. Staple onto large branches.

Attach arm branches to trunk through arm holds. Tape well. Flatten one end of each remaining large branch. Cut slits in trunk wide enough to allow flattened ends to pass through. Tape well to inside of trunk.

Add paper leaves. Cut slits to make walking easy.

If you place a tree cylinder around a chair, you will have a good hollow tree for an owl or an elf to hide in and pop up from when needed.

Birds

Fold tagboard in half.

Cut a beak at the front and round the head at the back.

Staple beak together and back of head at edge.

Add eyes and feathers.

Slip over head.

Add ties under chin.

Use corrugated paper with tagboard "straps" for wings (see page 31).

Tie tagboard feet onto shoes using laces.

Headbands

Cut a corrugated paper or tagboard strip long enough for a headband. Add desired features — ears, horns, etc.

Note: When working with corrugated paper, remember: for rigid things — keep ribs vertical; for floppy things — keep ribs horizontal.

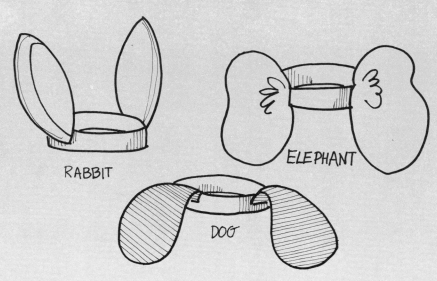

RABBIT

ELEPHANT

DOG

EASTER

BASKETS AND EGGS

Double Cone Basket

Fold a square piece of paper in half diagonally.

Hold with fold down and point up.

Bring A to B.

Overlap ends about 1" and staple.

Attach a paper strip handle to the two inner layers of paper. Decorate.

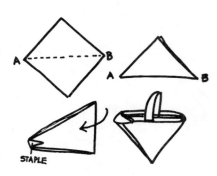

Woven Basket

Fold paper in half.

Cut through fold, but leave a generous border on the open edge. Don't cut all the way across (see A).

Weave one-inch strips through cuts. Glue or staple at each edge to secure weaving.

Treat the woven sheets as a regular piece of paper. Fold into thirds lengthwise, then open flat. Fold into thirds widthwise, then open flat again (see B). Fold up two adjoining sides (corner becomes a triangle, see C).

Glue or staple corner flat to lengthwise side (see D).

Repeat on other three corners.

Add handle and decorate (see E).

Note: For other styles of baskets, see pages 13 and 14.

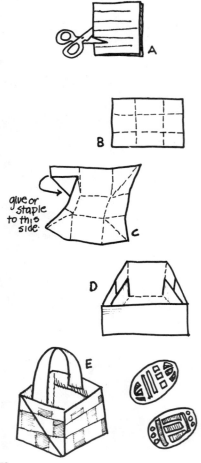

Mosaic Eggs

Cut large egg shapes from construction paper and then decorate with small squares of contrasting paper. Make tissue paper grass. Lay in basket with eggs.

Note: You could also glue small pieces of colored paper on real eggs.

RABBITS AND CHICKS

Use basic cone for heads or bodies (see page 33). Circles for the cones can be cut free-hand. Circles can also be zigzagged, fringed or scalloped.

Add features.

To use cone as body, add head, wings and legs or ears and cotton tail.

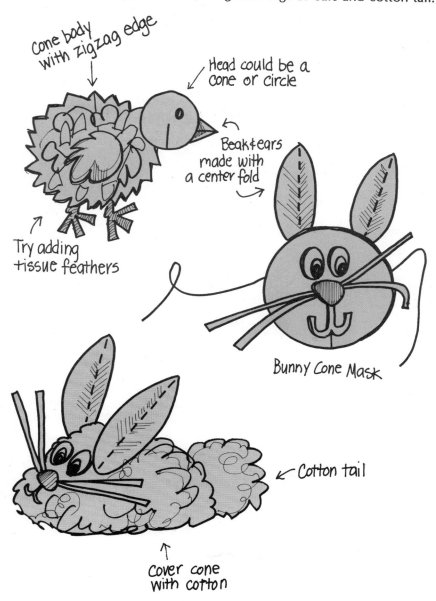

Cone body with zigzag edge

Head could be a cone or circle

Beak & ears made with a center fold

Try adding tissue feathers

Bunny Cone Mask

Cotton tail

Cover cone with cotton

ECOLOGY POSTERS

Decide on a slogan. Keep the message simple. Use cut-paper letters (see page 19).

Make a collage-style picture. Choose one or two things for impact.

Try using "found papers" for at least some of the design.

Make things stick out from poster by using folds, curls, slots.

For really big posters, glue to wrapping paper.

Ideas on what to say:

Save the trees	Save water
Pick up trash	Don't waste energy
Plant something green	Keep it natural

MAY
PAPIER-MÂCHÉ BUTTERFLIES

This project is good for symmetry concepts.

Fold paper in half. Draw butterfly wings and cut out. (Using this butterfly as a pattern, cut 4 or 5 more exactly the same.)

Using flour paste or thinned white glue, layer all butterfly shapes together. While still wet, prop up with crumpled balls of paper to shape. Let dry until hard, then remove the crumpled paper.

Decorate with tissue collage using thinned white glue.

Make matching designs for each wing.

Add curled or folded paper antenna.

Hang by threads.

Try balancing four or five butterflies in a mobile (see page 15).

For a large butterfly, use 4 or 5 sheets of newspaper. Commercial pinbacks may be glued on small butterflies with epoxy cement to make a pin.

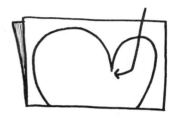

Make sure not to let this point go all the way to the fold.

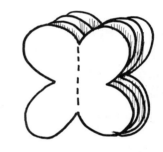

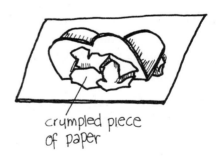

crumpled piece of paper

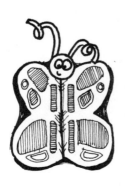

CHAIN CATERPILLARS

Use wide loops pasted into a chain the length desired. Then add features like eyes, feet, spots and fringe.

For a striped caterpillar, glue narrow strips onto wider strips before forming chain.

Tie on a string and pull.

Try making a snake of loops that get smaller and smaller.

LOOP BIRDS

Cut a long, wide strip of construction paper and roll it into a loop.

Add a base by making feet to glue on — a nice base could be heart-shaped, then cut to make toe shapes.

Make smaller loop for head.

Assemble with glue or staples.

Add beak, eyes, wings, and tail.

Hint: For adding eyes and wings, use a small strip of paper as a tab.

Add spots and stripes for markings.

Use appropriate colors for robins, bluebirds, crows, sparrows, etc., or make imaginary birds in wild colors.

TREE COLLAGE

Create trunk and branches from narrow cones. Keep in mind that trunk is large, while branches are medium to small. Make lots of branches.

Staple or glue to hold cones together. (Hold with paper clip if necessary.)

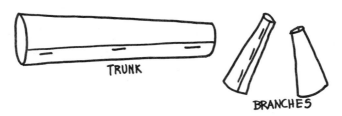

TRUNK

BRANCHES

Make a background of plain paper. Create a horizon by tearing a strip of another color for land.

Attach tree and branches to background with glue. Tear or cut leaves from scraps of colored paper, comics, or magazines, and "leaf" out your tree.

75

TIE-DYED PAPER NAPKIN FLOWERS

Put household liquid dyes in empty milk cartons.

Napkins come folded in quarters. Open up and bunch or fold either haphazardly or carefully. (You could also use paper towels.)

Clip here and there with snap clothespins.

Dip paper napkins into dye. Napkins will soak up dye instantly, so a short dip spreads dye rapidly.

Dip in various dyes.

Allow to dry thoroughly on newspaper before attempting to undo bundles. Iron out creases if desired, or you can leave the creases in as they add interest to finished flower.

To Make Flowers:

Refold napkins in quarters.

Cut an arc on the open edges to make circles. Scallop or point edge if desired. Each flower takes three to five napkins.

Twist each circle's centerpoint to make petals.

Use paper curls or strips for flower centers. Glue each petal at center, holding at twisted point.

Add stem by twisting or taping onto a chenille wire or coat hanger. Wind crepe paper around wire for a finished look.

Note: This same method can be used with colored tissue — just skip the dye bath.

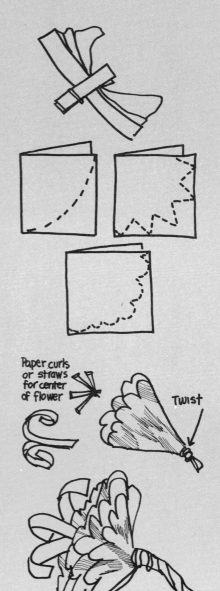

Paper curls or straws for center of flower

Twist

BOUQUETS

Make flower by folding paper and cutting out half a flower. Open paper.

Decorate centers. Paste flower tops to stems and leaves.

Make a dozen!

Add a paper bee or ladybug!

paper punch dots

Make some Loop Flowers, too.

Make center loop.

Make petal loops in different colors.

Try different sizes for petals.

Attach petal loops all around center loop.

Add stems and leaves.

Note: These make nice mobiles.

To give your bouquet to someone special, make a cone. (See page 33.)

Put stems of flowers inside.

Glue some flowers to inside edge if desired.

77

MOTHER'S DAY FLOWERS

For pattern, trace around hand carefully. Cut out one or more traced hands.

Glue into place on larger piece of paper as petals of a flower.

Cut out stem, leaves, stamen, and pistil. Try spirals, strips, etc.

Add a butterfly, caterpillar or ladybug.

CRAZY GARDEN MURAL

Trace around hands and feet. Use as flower and leaf parts. Cut out, using many colors. Paste to large sheet of paper. Make it as crazy as you can!

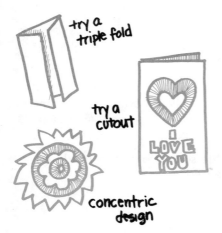

try a triple fold

try a cutout

concentric design

MOTHER'S DAY CARDS

Choose a message and/or a theme to use inside and out. Keep it simple but neat with special touches.

Try a scalloped edge or a pinked one.

Add a stripe of a different color.

Use a constrasting color inside the card on which to write your message.

Try concentric designs, each growing larger from a small center.

Letter your message in ink or paints.

GARDEN VEGETABLES MOBILES

Look at and talk about vegetables.

Cut paper shapes of a variety of vegetables. Use shallow cones for 3-D effect. (See page 33.)

Cut double so you can attach produce to strings.

Cut paper details.

Hang singly or make mobiles (see page 15). Remember, parts of a mobile must look good from both sides! sides!

FRAMED VEGETABLE PICTURES

Try many techniques:

Achieve a shadow box effect by using a lid to a shoe box or a shallow box. Cut three or four shapes of the same vegetable. Glue together placing a tiny cardboard spacer between each layer. Add details on top layer. Arrange in lid and glue in place.

Try paper sculpture of papier-mâché sealed with thinned white glue.

Or a small tissue collage of vegetables on cardboard or wood plaques. Drill small hole in wood for hanging.

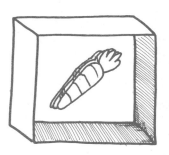

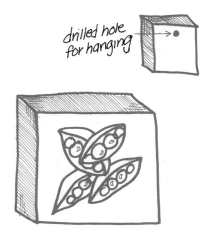

drilled hole for hanging

DANCING SCARECROWS

You can make scarecrows six inches or six feet tall.

Begin with paper rectangle for shirt body.

Add circle head with cutout features.

Use brown bags cut into fringe for straw.

Make long floppy arms and legs from strips folded accordion style and glued to body. Don't forget hands and feet — a little "straw" sticking out.

Make a few crows too.

Hang scarecrows around room or pin to bulletin board with heels kicked up.

JUNE — FATHER'S DAY
COLLAGE GREETING CARD

Make a special card by cutting words and small pictures from magazines and newspapers. Choose words or pictures that describe the person, the event, your feelings and/or the message. Make card background from colored paper or tagboard.

Glue words and pictures to background.

Design the cover like a beautiful puzzle, fitting words and pictures together until the front is filled. Try starting the arrangement with the two biggest words at angles like a "T", fitting in the others, overlapping only when necessary.

Add little extras like fabric, foil, ribbon snips, etc.

Use cut-paper words or letters for inside message, too!

Try a cutout in cover so that some of inside message can be seen.

81

CITY MURAL

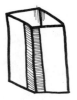

Make an imaginary city you'd like to visit or a map of your own community.

Make basic building shape by folding each side to center (see page 13). Make as many as you need for your city.

Decorate front with colored windows in rows. Do this very carefully. Add doors, shop fronts, apartments, etc.

Connect building shapes with small pieces of construction paper and tape.

Staple to bulletin board. Add planes, antennaes, street lights, cars and paper people.

Try covering large cardboard boxes with wrapping paper to use as buildings — set up as a city to walk around.

TRANSPORTATION

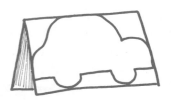

Make basic body shapes for cars, trailers, campers, and trucks by folding paper and drawing outline of vehicle.

Cut out, leaving the folded edge uncut.

Cut out and glue on windows, windshields, tires, doors, and bumpers.

Add people's faces cut from construction paper or photos from magazines and glue in the windows.

Set up on base or a road map background.

Try this technique for planes, too!

STUFFED FORM INSECTS

Fold wrapping paper in half and draw and cut out a basic insect shape (you'll have a front and a back). Keep shapes large and simple.

Glue together, leaving 6" x 8" opening in seam for stuffing. Crumpled newspaper works fine as stuffing. After stuffing, glue rest of seam together.

Add features — legs, spots, heads, etc.

String to hang.

These forms could be stuffed with candy and used as piñatas!

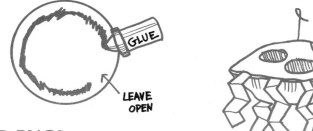

3-D BUGS

Decide on bug shape. Then choose a paper sculpture shape that best fits the desired effect and cut it out.

Try symmetrical designs.

Cut a slit and overlap a little to make a 3-D form.

Add legs, spots, heads and antenna.

Make short folded paper springs and use to attach wings to body so they will wiggle. Wings can be circles or rounded triangles.

For a fuzzy look, try torn strips of paper.

Make big leaves for a background on which to place bugs.

Remember — insects have 6 legs; spiders have 8.

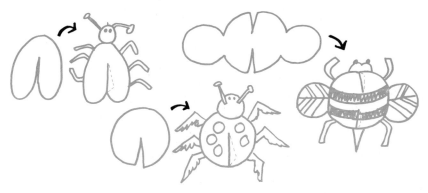

FROG PRINCE

Loop a rectangular piece of paper over and glue edges.

Trim corners to make a curve.

Add spots (use waste paper from a paper punch).

Cut four feet.

Don't forget webbed toes!

Make four legs using the spring technique or simpler accordion strip (see pages 11 and 12).

Attach feet to legs; legs to body.

Add eyes. Try circles inside of larger circles. Fool around with pupils.

Try attaching eyes to body with short accordion strips to let eyes wiggle.

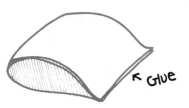

Use to make an attractive underwater bulletin board.

3-D FISH

Draw and cut out basic body shape which can be as simple as a circle or a long oval.

Cut slit to center.

Overlap sides on either side of the slit making a shallow cone. Staple or glue in place.

Decorate with appropriate eyes, fins, spots, stripes, etc.

Try decorating with tissue scales cut out and overlapped. Brush thinned white glue on tissue.

POP-UP NATURE PICTURES

To make anything pop-up and wiggle, use two strips of paper identical in size and shape.

Glue together to form a "**1**" shape, then fold the "**1**" shapes back and forth across each other until desired length is reached (see page 12). Glue ends.

Attach a cutout so that it can wiggle on one end while the other end is attached to the background.

Try cutouts of flowers, trees, bees, butterflies, birds, horses, and so on. Use cut-paper or tissue collage to make background.

Try using newspaper want ads for gray mountains, or cut parts of pictures from a lawn and garden section in a magazine for stems and grass.

VACATIONLAND DIORAMAS

Choose a box. (See page 16.) Cover inside of box with appropriate colors for the display desired.

Think of your scene in parts. The sky first, then land background — the farthest away items, then closer things, such as trees, rocks, people, cars, animals.

Add a row of standup things in the flat background by cutting out shape, bending flap on bottom and gluing in box. Add cars, people or animals using paper sculpture techniques.

Diorama can have cellophane or plastic wrap across top with peep hole to look in from front, or box can be left open in front as shown in the illustration.

TRAVEL POSTERS

Choose a place to visit and decide on a picture "symbol" that illustrates that place.

Cut out a rectangle for each letter of the name of the place. Keep letters all the same size (try different colors). (See page 19.)

Use paper sculpture techniques to make an illustration for the poster — keep it large, bold, and simple: one large image is easier to see and remember.

Paste and hang.

Arrange lettering across rather than trying fancy things (like vertical or diagonal) — makes it easy to read!

JULY — FOURTH OF JULY
PARADE COSTUMES

Patriotic themes are fun.

Look up a famous person for ideas on what you need for your costumes. Invent ways to make paper work for what you need as props. See pages 30-34, 50-51 and 68-69 for costume-making techniques. Alter or modify pieces to fit your character.

Tricorn Hat

Cut hole in paper to fit head.

Pinch and staple to form Corners 1 and 2. Pinch to form Corner 3. Adjust to fit head if necessary. Staple.

Note: If hole is too small, continue cutting until fit is achieved.

Add rossette cockade if desired.

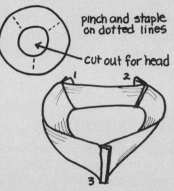

Crepe-Paper Wig

Make paper headband as base.

Attach crepe paper to band, gathering gently at front.

Let sides taper down and tie with paper bow.

Side curls can be rolled and glued on band.

Cap

Cut a large crepe-paper circle.

Use large running stitches to gather into "Betsy Ross" cap.

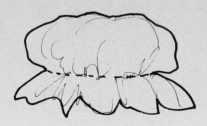

SPORTS POSTERS

Decide on a team name or a special player. Use cut-paper letters (see page 19).

Make a picture collage of a player in action or the team symbol or mascot.

Paste to a colorful background. Use your team's colors.

Try using cutouts from sports magazines for background or for part of the image — perhaps a well-known face on a cut-paper body.

CIRCUS PUPPETS

TRAPEZE
STAR

Use a small stuffed paper bag for the basic form (see page 29). Tape or tie neck, leaving room for fingers to go into head.

Add face, arms, legs, paws, ears and costumes to create character desired. Use paper scraps.

CLOWN

LION

How about — Lion tamer, Ringmaster, Bareback rider, Balloon man.

DAISY CHAIN NECKLACE

Cut many small flower and leaf shapes. Add centers to flowers. Add veins to leaves if desired.

Ways To Connect:

Cut short strips for stems. Glue to backs of flowers and leaves. Make chain by gluing stems into loops and interlocking them.

Or glue one stem to the back of the next flower making straight connection.

Or use a string for the necklace, gluing the flowers in place with a little square of paper.

TISSUE FLOWER GARLAND

Cut squares of tissue about 4" x 4" for small flowers.

Fold in half and cut flower shapes. Open up and twist each petal in center.

Do many sheets at once to speed up things.

Glue three or four petals around a pipe-cleaner stem.

Make as many flowers as needed to make a flower crown.

Twist pipe cleaners together until garland is the right size.

Glue on paper leaves.

Add ribbon, bows and streamers.

Glue around pipe-cleaner stem

89

AUGUST
SUN MOBILES

Talk about radiating colors and shapes and ways to make parts stick out (See pages 12, 73, 79, 84 and 85). Experiment with different papers (magazine pages, aluminum foil, cellophane, foil wrapping paper, tissue). Look for unusual color combinations.

Construct basic shape of cones, loops, and stuffed forms.

Attach rays with glue or staples.

Attach string and hang.

Consider hanging parts within shapes.

Try balancing many small suns in one big mobile (see page 15).

Make paper sun piñata to celebrate summer. Fill with treats.

Cut slits in opposite sides of cylinders. Cut corresponding slits in circles. Slip cylinders on edge of circle. Tape circle tab to inside of cylinder.

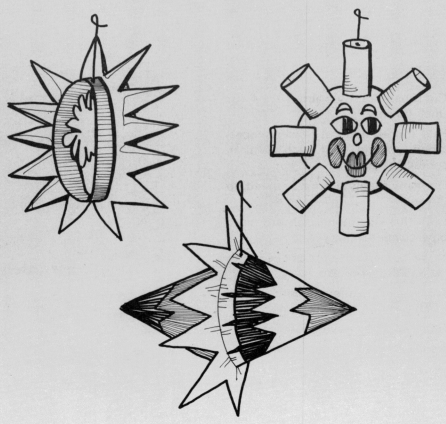

PLEATED PAPER FAN

Take a sheet of colored paper at least 9″ x 12″.

Pleat accordion style by folding lengthwise.

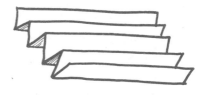

If a scalloped edge is desired, open up and cut scallops between each fold line, or try cutting one scallop with paper folded.

Find center and fold in half, taping the two joining ends together.

Larger fans are made from larger paper.

Decorate with cut-paper strips and shapes. Try adding a ribbon or yarn handle.

For a lacy look, snip tiny shapes out of the folded edges.

SCALLOPED EDGE

DOG DAYS

Begin with a cylinder of paper. Staple or tape.

Cut a long oval, circle or triangle to use for head. Attach to one end of cylinder. (You may have to cut a curve in cylinder's end to fit head.)

Cut eyes, ears, tail, nose, and tongue.

Glue tabs inside bottom of cylinder for feet.

Use eyebrows to change expressions. Make a large nose on a big dog; little ears on a fat dog, etc. Make a dog you know and love.

Make a doghouse on a bulletin board.

Staple dogs all over or set on a counter.

How about a cat?

TURTLE RACE

Begin with shallow cone body (see page 33).
Cut out four legs by folding paper twice and cutting once.

Cut out a head with a neck shape and a tail.
Add eyes (don't forget pupils).
Attach all parts and decorate shell with cutout patterns.
Make your turtle special. (Does it have a name?)
Punch a hold in center of face. Attach a long string through hole.
Pull to make turtle run.
Try winding string around a wide strip of cardboard.
The one who reels the fastest WINS!

RODEO HORSES

Begin with a cardboard box big enough to stand in and to pull up around hips.

Cut off top and bottom of box.

Attach twine suspenders by puncturing holes in both sides of box and knotting twine. Try on to adjust length. You may want to cross straps in back. Paint box or cover with paper of desired color. Torn paper makes pinto spots.

Using flaps removed for box opening, staple or glue one at right angles to another. Trim to create horse's head. Fold paper and cut to form ears.

Add paper fringe mane and tail. Fold to make double thick fringe.

Add ears, eyes and bridle with reins.

Cut slit in box as deep as horse's neck. Widen to accomodate thickness of cardboard. Slide head in slit. Tape to inside of box.

94

INDEX